For Deniz

© Copyright 2014

Written by Sally A Jones and Amanda C Jones
Illustrations by Annalisa C Jones

Published by GUINEA PIG EDUCATION

2 Cobs Way,
New Haw,
Addlestone,
Surrey,
KT15 3AF.
www.guineapigeducation.co.uk

NO part of this publication may be reproduced, stored or copied for commercial purposes and profit without the prior written permission of the publishers.

ISBN: 978-1-907733-84-0

Dear Kids and Parents,

This book contains a structured course to teach children to spell using phonics.

A friendly character, an alien called Zoggy, encourages your child to work hard to achieve good results in spelling... just as a sportsman trains hard to keep fit. In order to achieve this, he teaches ten important spelling rules: including, doubling middle sounds; adding endings; plurals; and homophones.

Each challenge includes funny phonic rhymes, phrases and sentences to reinforce the sounds being taught; learn them off by heart, practise rewriting them from memory. There are also a series of exercises to help your child practise spelling, including tests where your child can read, copy, cover and spell. In addition, this book contains extensive lists of words with more complex endings that your child can practise.

MEET Zoggy...

ZOGGY has been sent from planet ZEN, three million light years away.

ZOGGY'S FIRST CHALLENGE

REPORT BACK TO PLANET ZEN...

Earthlings practise lots of sports to <u>keep fit.</u> <u>They train hard every day.</u> In the same way <u>you</u> need to work hard to achieve good results in spelling.

"Let's get training!"

Which one?

a athletics	**b** basketball badminton	**c** canoeing	**d** diving discus
e equestrian sports	**f** football fencing	**g** games	**h** hockey horse riding high jump
i ice skating	**j** judo	**k** karate kayaking	**l** long jump
m martial arts motor racing mountaineering	**n** net ball	**o** orienteering	**p** pentathlon ping pong polo
qu quad biking	**r** rowing	**s** swimming surfing sailing	**t** tennis table tennis
u underwater sports	**v** volleyball	**w** weightlifting water skiing	**x** make up a zen sport
y yachting	**z** zorbing		

Zoggy says,

"Find a simple word for each sound."

DOUBLE INITIAL SOUNDS

cl	fl	pl	sl	sc	sk	spl	sm	sn
clap	flap	play			skip	splash		

fr	tr	cr	pr	ect	ch	sh	wh	th
					church			

MIDDLE SOUNDS

oo	ee	ar	or	ur	ir	er
		park				faster

oa	ai	ay	oi	oy	e

MIDDLE SOUNDS

ce	ci	cy	ge	gi	gy

ow	oa	ow	ou	ue	ew
row	boat	crown	shout		

au	aw
taught	lawn

"Just a few more to go..."

TRIPLE INITIAL SOUNDS

scr	spr	shr	spl	str	sph	tch
scream	spray	shred	splash	street	sphere	fetch
						scratch

Zoggy has a go at:

football

'oo'

Zoggy has a go at:

archery

'ar'   'ch'

Zoggy takes up some sporting challenges.

ai   oa

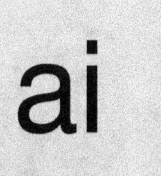

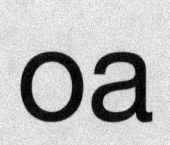

I am:

S AI L ING

not failing

B OA T ING

and floating.

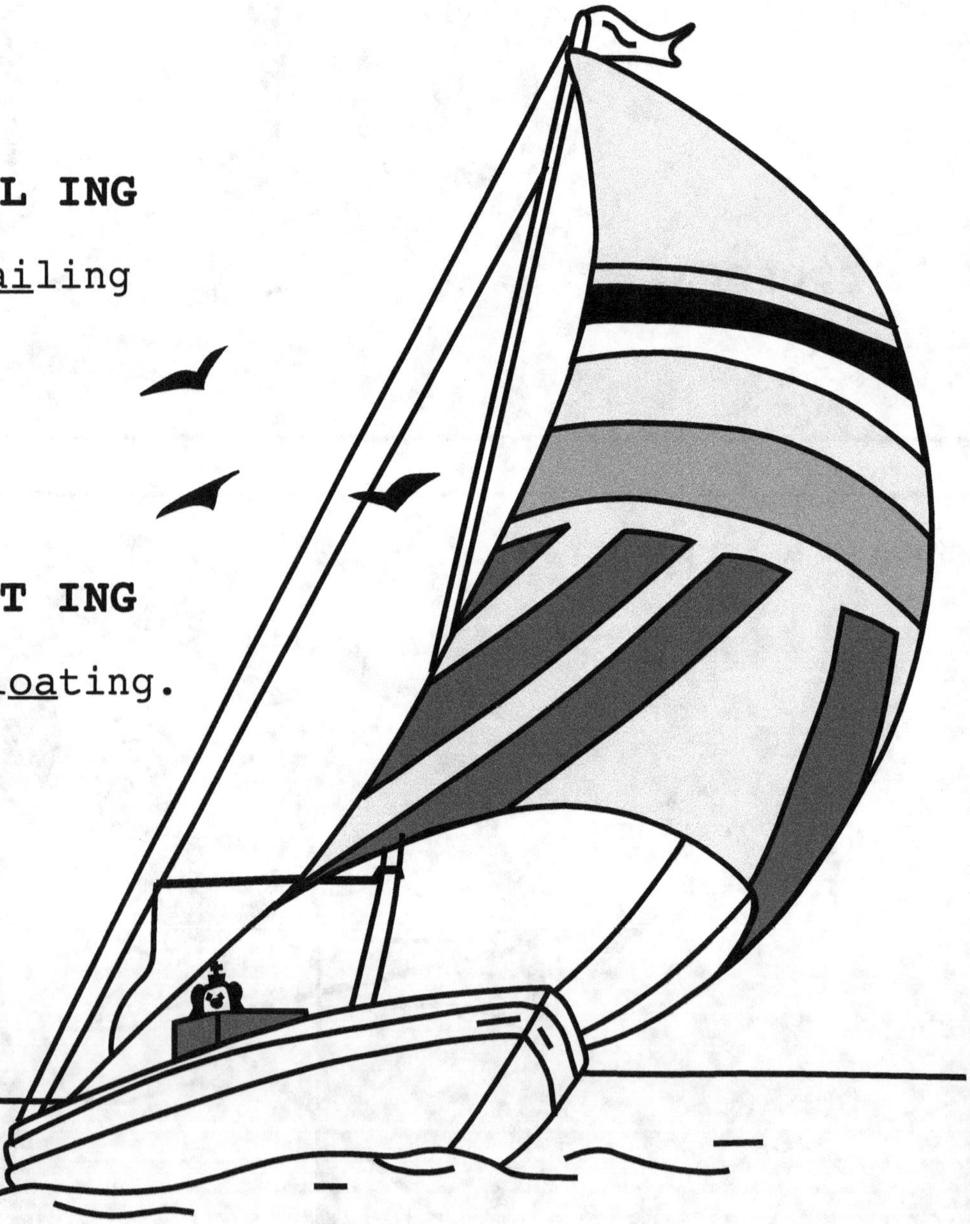

Use phonics to sound out words.

He goes...

z<u>o</u>rbing

He jumps the...

h<u>ur</u>dles

goes

s<u>ur</u>fing,

wak<u>e</u> b<u>oar</u>ding

and

sh<u>ow</u> jumping.

What do you think Zoggy?

More sporting challenges for Zoggy to take up...

Draw Zoggy's adventures.

F**OO**TBALL HOT AIR BALLOONING	CHESS FREE FALLING	KITE SURFING
PENTATHLON ATHLETICS	ZORBING	*Make up Zoggy's favourite* ZEN SPORT - *IR*
WHITE WATER RAFTING SOCCER	HURDLE CURLING	ARCHERY
SHOOTING SNOOKER	SHOW JUMPING ROWING SNOW BOARDING	POWER BOATING

Find these sounds: ch, sh, wh, th, oo, ee, ar, or, ur, ir, er, silent e

TRAWLING TO CATCH FISH	WAKE BOARDING	AUTOMATIC CAR RACING
RUGBY SKY DIVING	SAILING RELAY RACE	QUOITS
MOUNTAIN CLIMBING ROUNDERS	CANAL BOATING	CLAY PIGEON SHOOTING

e'   cut   cute

'e' jumps back and makes the vowel short.

ai	ay	oi	oy
oa	ow	ay	aw
long y	short y		

CHALLENGE TWO

Zoggy takes up some sporting challenges.

- running
- swimming
- tennis
- volleyball

LEARN

SPELLING RULE NUMBER ONE

Zoggy says,

"WHEN THERE IS A SHORT VOWEL SOUND IN A VERB LIKE RUN, YOU USUALLY DOUBLE THE CONSONANT 'RUNNING'. CAN YOU HEAR THE STRESS IN THE SECOND CONSONANT?"

When Zoggy plays tennis, the ball is spi<u>nn</u>ing but he is gri<u>nn</u>ing.

Zoggy is ru<u>nn</u>ing a race, but keeping up the pace.

He is swi<u>mm</u>ing in my lane and winning again.

Zoggy plays te<u>nn</u>is again with De<u>nn</u>is.

Which sport does he like the best? Vo<u>ll</u>ey ball... No! I love them all.

Zoggy says, "Double the consonants in these verbs where appropriate."

ROOT WORDS	...ing	...ed	...er
hop			
hug			
slim			
skip			
rip			
shop			
trim			
jog	jogging	jogged	jogger
bet			
fit			
pat			
tug			
drag			
slip			
grab			
clap			
rub			
trip			

Remember, if a one syllable word ends in a single vowel, you need to double the consonant before adding an ending e.g. sit   sitting.

Can you hear a stress on the second 't'?

Let's look at these adjectives.

Do you need to double the consonant?

ROOT WORD	COMPARATIVE add er	SUPERLATIVE add est
hot	hotter	hottest
slim		
big		
fat		
thin		

Time for a test.

READ	COPY	COVER & SPELL
swimming		
carriage		
running		
beginning		
million		
canning		
fanning		
stopping		
slipping		
sunny		
trapped		
skipping		
carefully		
actually		
hopped		
grabbed		
trimming		
dropped		
gradually		
challenging		

READ	COPY	COVER & SPELL
scrapped		
planned		
matting		
spotted		
rubbing		
stopping		
clapped		
rolling		
hopping		

"Remember, words with short vowel sounds usually double the consonants: swim, begin, rub, hop, grab, mat, slip, hit, sit.."

"Listen for a stressed sound. Say it hop**P**ing."

CHALLENGE THREE

Zoggy goes...　　　　DIV~~E~~　　　DIV<u>ING</u>　　　　in the pool.

"The water is really cool."

LEARN

SPELLING RULE NUMBER TWO

Zoggy says,

"WHEN YOU ADD A SUFFIX, LIKE 'ING', TO A VERB ENDING WITH A VOWEL, THE 'E' IS DROPPED. THE 'I' WORKS LIKE 'E' AND YOU DO NOT NEED BOTH OF THEM."

ICE SKATE

I am **ice skating** in the rink, slipping and sliding, I think.

HORSE RIDE

I am **riding** on my horse, holding on the reigns tight of course.

Zoggy says, "fill in the chart,"

ROOT WORDS	...ing	...ed	...er
hope	hoping	hoped	hoper
hide			
ride			
collide			
stride			
slide			
glide			
rake			
bake			
take			
bike			
snake			
race			
trace			
skate			
wipe			
state			
swipe			
like			
fine			

Remember: to add a suffix like 'ing' to a verb, drop 'e' - bake   baking

Look what happens to these adjectives

ROOT WORD	Drop e to add er	Drop e to add est
safe	safer	safest
wide		
ripe		
close		
nice		

Look what happens to verbs.

To double 'k' put 'ck' - 'jacket'.

ROOT WORD	...ing	...ed	...er
lick			
trick			
stick			
rack			
unlock			
stack			
truck			
panic	panicking	panicked	
back			
munch			
bunch			
wish			
fish			
vanish			
fetch			
bath			

Time for a test.

READ	COPY	COVER & SPELL
hope		
hoping		
arrive		
arrived		
stripe		
striped		
require		
required		
explore		
exploring		
rehearse		
rehearsing		
involve		
involved		
sense		
sensing		
include		
including		
surprise		
surprising		
excite		
excited		
stripes		
striped		

READ	COPY	COVER & SPELL
escape		
escaping		
have		
having		
bake		
baking		
decide		
deciding		
wipe		
wiping		
use		
using		
secure		
secured		
refuse		
refusing		
come		
coming		
care		
caring		
arrive		
arrived		
love		
loved		

Remember:

1. 'i' works like 'e' so when you add 'ing', 'er' or 'ed' drop the 'e'
2. A, E, I, O, U are long sounds so drop the 'e'.

In fact, drop the final 'e' in all words, if an ending begins with a vowel.

ROOT WORD		
expense	expens	ive
refuse	refus	al
love	lov	able
fame	fam	ous
shine	shin	y

Which ending?

arrive	excite	expanse	danger	shine
ous	al	able	ive	y

(excite → able)

TIME FOR A TEST

Fill in the chart, making words where appropriate:

ROOT WORDS	ing	ed	er	y	al	able
trim						
quack						
hope						
love						
run						
wake						
refuse						
win	winning	×	winner	×	×	×
scrub						
excite						
fish						
admit						
stretch						
arrive						
shine						
kiss						
remove						

LEARN

SPELLING RULE NUMBER THREE

Zoggy says,

"DROP THE FINAL 'E' IF A WORD ENDS IN 'LE' AND ADD 'Y'."

What do you think of white water rafting, Zoggy?

Simple!
Simply amazing

Comfortable
I must sit comfortably

Possible
It is possibly risky

Struggle
I am struggling to get the hang of it

Grumble
I'll be grumbling if I fall in.

Tremble
I feel trembly!

SPLASH!!!

LEARN

SPELLING RULE NUMBER FOUR

Zoggy says,

"IF A WORD ENDS IN TWO OR MORE SYLLABLES, ADD 'ILY'.

How do you feel Zoggy?

"Happy..."

"I am steadily making my way along the river in my rowing boat, paddling busily and singing merrily."

Zoggy is happy. He paddles happily along.

The raft is steady. It travels steadily along the rapids.

Zoggy is busy. He is busily paddling with the oars.

He is merry. He sings merrily to himself.

CHALLENGE FIVE

> LEARN
>
> **SPELLING RULE NUMBER FIVE**
>
> Zoggy says,
>
> "IF A WORD ENDS IN 'LL', JUST ADD 'Y'.

Shrill ⟶ Cry out **shrilly**

Full ⟶ **Fully** soaked

CHALLENGE SIX

> LEARN
>
> **SPELLING RULE NUMBER SIX**
>
> Zoggy says,
>
> "IF A WORD ENDS IN SS, SH, CH, X, OR ZZ ADD 'ES' FOR VERBS AND PLURALS."

What sporting challenge shall I take up now to learn 'es'?

Wasps buzz. A wasp buzzes.

Foxes watch. A fox watches.

A horse travels in a horse box. Horses travel in horse boxes.

Swimmers splash. A swimmer splashes.

Zoggy takes a riding class. He takes riding classes.

CHALLENGE SEVEN

Zoggy rides his pony.
He rides ponies.

He gallops across the country.
He gallops across countries

He gallops across the valley
He gallops across valleys.

Zoggy is busy.
He busies himself.

Zoggy is in a hurry.
He hurries to the stable.

A van brings a supply of food.
It supplies food.

REMEMBER

SPELLING RULE NUMBER SEVEN

Zoggy says,

"FOR WORDS ENDING IN A CONSONANT AND 'Y', ADD 'IES'. FOR EXAMPLE, SATISFY - SATISFIED (VERB) AND PONY - PONIES (PLURALS). BUT IF A WORD ENDS IN A VOWEL AND 'Y' ADD 'S' (DONKEY, DONKEYS)."

CHALLENGE EIGHT

LEARN

SPELLING RULE NUMBER EIGHT

ZOGGY TEACHES YOU TO MAKE MORE WORDS PLURAL:

1. IF A WORD ENDS IN 'F', 'FF', OR 'FE' ADD 'S' OR 'VES'
2. IF A WORD ENDS IN AN 'O' ADD 'ES'

The horse stops to munch a berry.
He munches on berries.

The pony eats a leaf.
He eats leaves.

He can carry his riding kit.
He carries his kit.

The pony hurt a hoof.
He hurt his hooves.

A tomato plant is growing in the garden.
Tomatoes are growing.

Read these rules again...

Remember:

To make most words plural, just add 's'

but...

Add 'es' to words ending in 'ch', 'sh', 'ss', 's' or 'x'	classes		
If the word ends in a consonant and 'y', drop the 'y' and add 'ies'	qualify qualifies	city cities	ruby rubies
Words ending in vowels and 'y' add 's'	monkey monkeys	donkey donkeys	
If the word ends in a 'o' add 'es'	tomato tomatoes	potato potatoes	
If the word ends in 'lf' add 'ves' or 's'	ourself ourselves		

Remember, there are exceptions to the rule:

handkerchief - handkerchiefs   *belief - beliefs*

Some words take on a new word:

woman - women   *foot - feet*   *ox - oxen*   *mouse - mice*

Some words stay the same:

sheep   *trout*

Now, practise these endings.

ROOT WORD adjective	COMPARATIVE drop Y add ier	SUPERLATIVE drop Y add iest	ADVERB drop Y add ily
lazy	lazier	laziest	lazily
busy			
hungry			
funny			
happy			
shabby			
merry			
steady			
happy			
sleepy			
clumsy			
silly			
prickly			
lucky			
friendly			
noisy			
pretty			
stormy			
steady			
tricky			
nasty			
early			
lovely			
weary			
messy			

What happens when you build up these words?

ROOT WORD	Add ...ness
ill	illness
dark	
stark	
blind	
fit	
sad	

ROOT WORD	Add ...'ly'
brave	bravely
slow	
loud	
cruel	
true	

ROOT WORD	Add 'i' and add ...ness
happy	happiness
silly	
nasty	
clumsy	
saucy	

ROOT WORD	Add ...able
enjoy	enjoyable
accept	
comfort	
reason	

ROOT WORD	Remove 'e'
value	valuable
achieve	
admire	
love	
excuse	
believe	
manage	

Sort these adjectives:

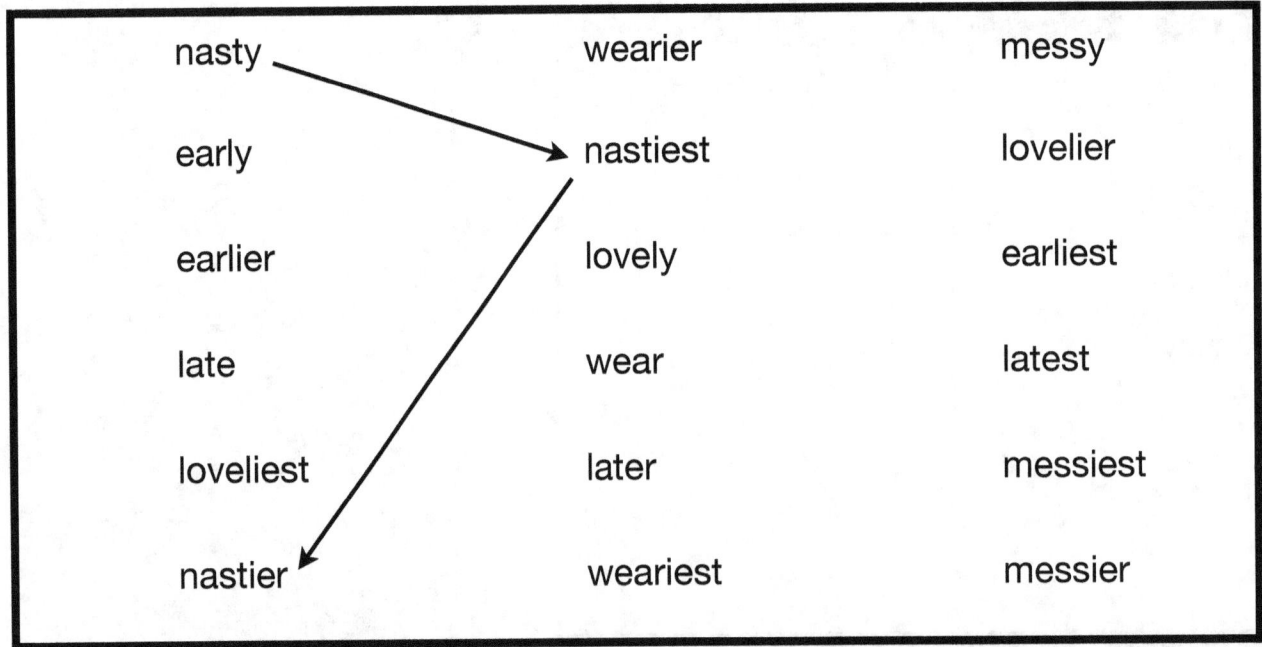

Can you find more examples?

ADJECTIVE	COMPARATIVE	SUPERLATIVE
lovely	lovelier	loveliest

These words are formed in other ways:

ADJECTIVE	COMPARATIVE	SUPERLATIVE
good	better	best
beautiful	more beautiful	most beautiful

CHALLENGE NINE

LEARN

SPELLING RULE NUMBER NINE

Zoggy says,

1. "<u>GE</u>, <u>GI</u> AND <u>GY</u> HAVE A SOFT SOUND LIKE 'J'.

    GYMNASTICS

2. <u>CE</u>, <u>CI</u> AND <u>CY</u> HAVE A SOFT 'C' SOUND LIKE 'S'

    ICE SKATING

    BUT THE 'C' IN CAT IS A HARD SOUND."

Zoggy says,

"A walk in space is ACE."

When 'c' comes before a consonant or the vowels a, o, u it sounds like 'k'. Some words have a double 'c'.

A**cc**ept, a**cc**ident and su**cc**ess have a hard 'c' and a soft 'c'

Can you hear the hard 'c' and the soft 'c'?

Time for a test.

READ	COPY	COVER & SPELL
fence		
place		
dance		
audience		
December		
pencil		
bicycle		
ambulance		
anticipation		
participation		
accident		
exciting		
centre		
century		
recent		
except		
scissors		
cylinder		
produce		
difference		
scenery		
special		

"Remember, when you have 'cc', the first 'c' is hard like 'k' and the second 'c' is soft like 's'."

| succeed | accept | success | accelerate |
| accent | access | accident | accustom |

"Remember 'cess'…"

| process | success | princess | recess |
| access | abscess | necessary | |

"Remember, short words end in 'ck' (pack).

"In long words ending in this sound 'ck' is 'c'."

| panic | picnic | frantic | mimic |
| logic | fantastic | arithmetic | |

Time for a test.

Soft g, ge, gi and gy

READ	COVER & SPELL
village	
danger	
huge	
energy	
engine	
digital	
gymnastics	
ginger	
large	
George	
hinge	
plunge	
orange	
change	
edge	
badge	
allergy	
bridge	
budget	
judge	
sledge	
manage	
damage	
garage	
passage	
guide	
guilty	

READ	COVER & SPELL
luggage	
edge	
suggest	
challenging	
zoology	
guinea pig	
Egypt	
stranger	
strange	
energetic	
engage	
magic	
tragic	
gipsy	
imagine	
fudge	
fringe	
hedge	
storage	
bandage	
largest	
gentleman	
register	
gentle	
guitar	
guess	
gymnast	

"Remember: when you have 'ge', 'gi' or 'gy', the 'g' sound is soft as in 'j'.

When 'g' is before a, o or u it sounds like 'g'."

Zoggy talks to the manager about registering for the gym.

It looks challenging. Will he have enough energy?

Find words for these tricky sounds.

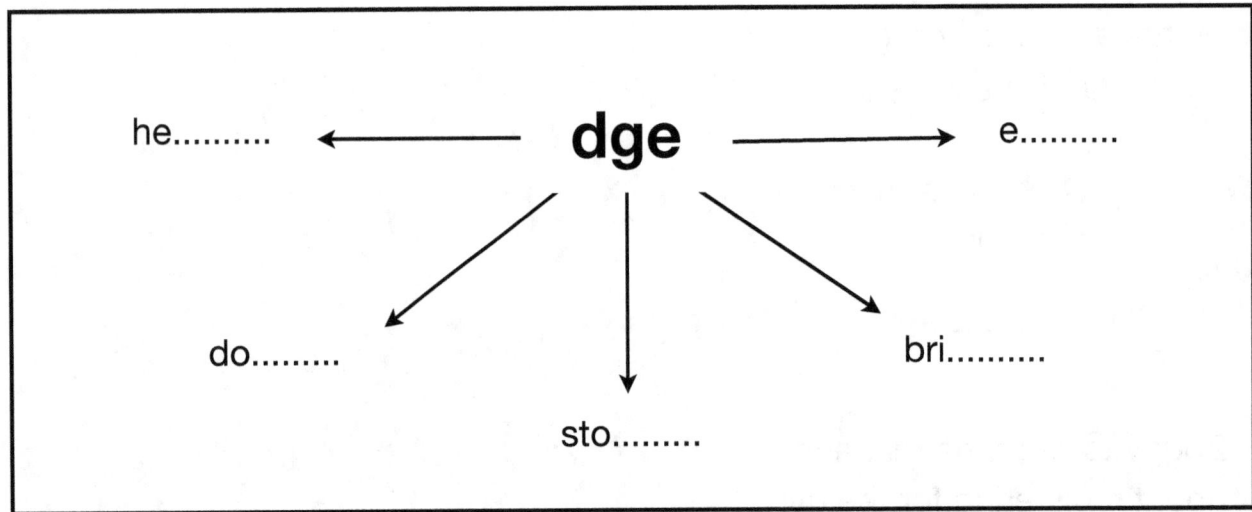

he.......... ← **dge** → e..........
do......... ↙ ↓ ↘ bri..........
sto.........

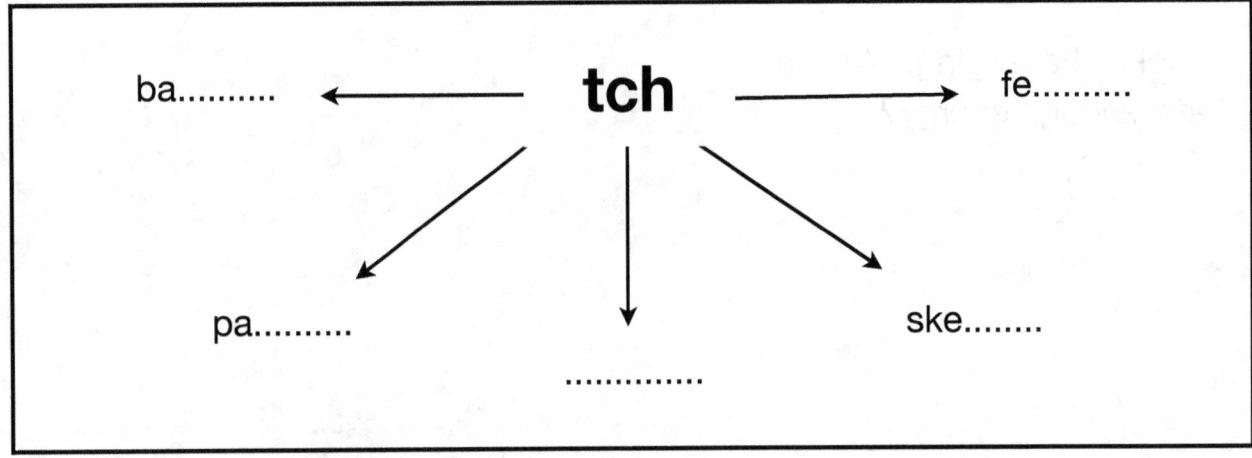

ba.......... ← **tch** → fe..........
pa.......... ↙ ↓ ↘ ske........
....

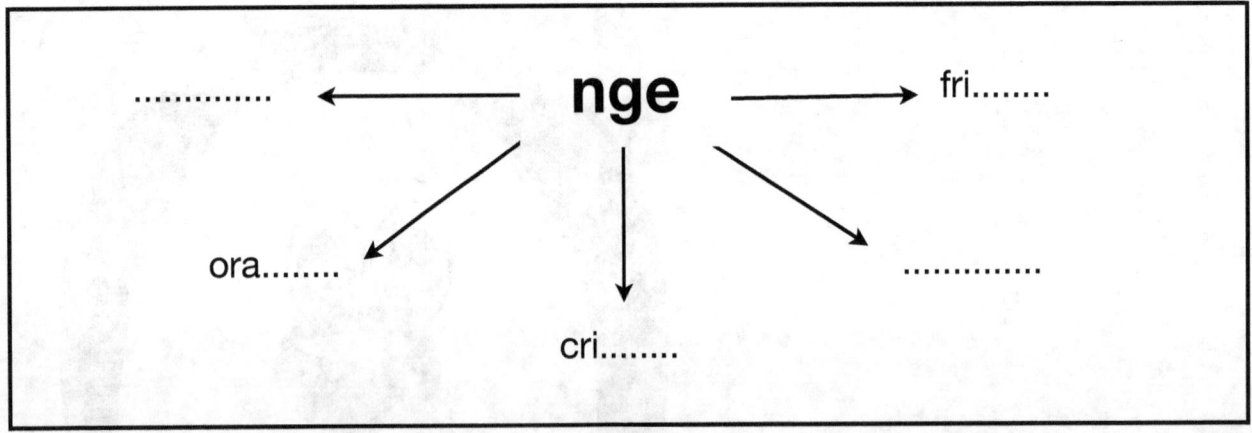

.... ← **nge** → fri........
ora........ ↙ ↓ ↘ ....
cri........

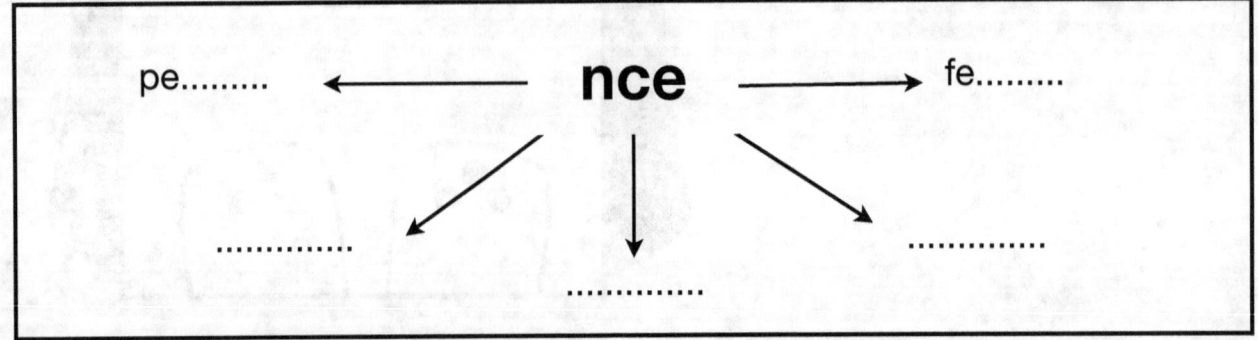

pe......... ← **nce** → fe.........
.... ↙ ↓ ↘ ....
....

CHALLENGE TEN

SPELLING RULE NUMBER TEN

Zoggy says,

"ROOT WORDS NEVER CHANGE WHEN YOU ADD A PREFIX."

Zoggy is an alien so he can make things **appear** and then **disappear** using his special powers from Planet Zen.

Create new words by matching the correct prefixes to the root words below.

| pre | ex | mis | intr | bi | ex | be | dis | tre | com |
| em | in | pro | pre | re | un | tri | bi | sub | non |

verse	appear	popular	afraid
understand	angle	cycle	spelling
satisfied	turn	trust	vent
necessary	calm	way	sense

unafraid

....

....

....

....

....

Zoggy takes up a sporting challenge on the track and he takes part in a cycle race on his bicycle.

Is he afraid?
Certainly not, he is unafraid.

Is he a popular member of the team?
No, he is unpopular.

Why?
He cheats using his special powers to get to the front of the race.

Is he satisfied with the result?
No, he is dissatisfied.

Why?
He does not win because he falls off his bike.

SPELLING RULE NUMBER ELEVEN

Zoggy says,

"IN MOST WORDS THE ROOT WORD DOES NOT CHANGE WHEN YOU ADD A SUFFIX LIKE 'LY'."

Zoggy takes up a sporting challenge in the gym.

"Oh! A balance beam. How exciting..."

His back flip is beautiful.
He performs it beautifully.

He has no fear.
He is fearless.

Take care Zoggy!
Be careful!

Match the suffixes to the words below. You can use them more them once and may have to drop letters.

| less | ly | ness | ed | ful | ing | able |

use	near	beauty
fear	hope	enjoy
bright	care	race

BEAUTIFUL
Long words have a single consonant.

FALL
Short words have a double consonant.

SUFFIXES: look at these verbs.

"'i' works like 'e', you do not need both"

tire	+	ed	→	tired
ripe	+	est	→	ripest
wake	+	ing	→	waking

"doubling rule"

dip	+p	ing	→	dipping
slim	+m	ing	→	slimming

wise	+	ly	→	wisely
use	+	ful	→	useful
tire	+	some	→	tiresome
care	+	less	→	careless

Time for a test.

READ	COPY	COVER & SPELL
unbearably		
although		
building		
disguised		
unsure		
regardless		
throughly		
unusual		
hopeful		
camped		
gradually		

Revision

Double the consonant if a word has one syllable, short vowel and ends in a consonant.

"Fun... so fu**nn**y."

"Stop... I am sto**pp**ing."

Can you hear a stress on the second 'p'?

There are exceptions to this rule: marketing, targeting

CHALLENGE ELEVEN

LEARN

SPELLING RULE NUMBER TWELVE

Zoggy says,

"'I' BEFORE 'E' EXCEPT AFTER 'C' BUT ONLY WHEN THE SOUND IS 'EE'..."

On the **field**, he tries javelin, discus, shot, high jump and long jump.

Will he **receive** a medal?

There are always a few exceptions.

"Have I cleared the **height**?"

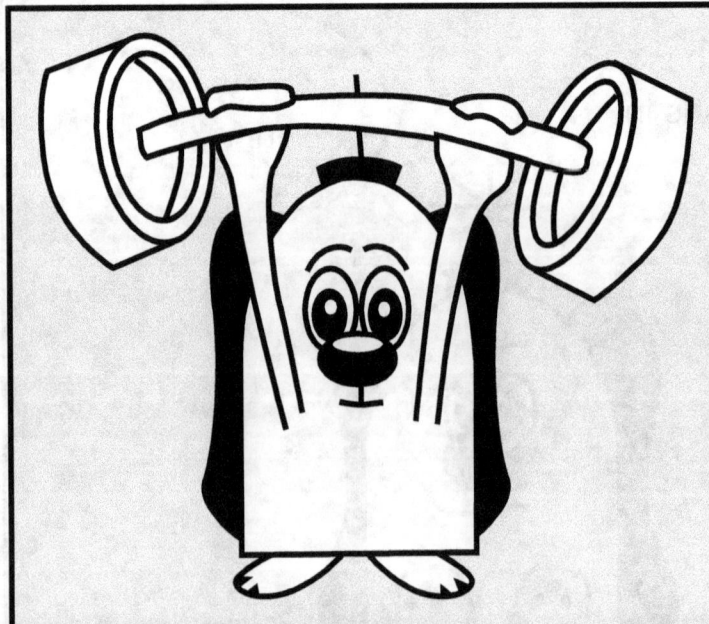

Zoggy goes to the **leisure** centre to try weight lifting.

Time for a test.

READ	COPY	COVER & SPELL
field		
retrieve		
yield		
chief		
relief		
grief		
believing		
piece		
deceive		
heights		
eight		
weight		
sleigh		
neigh		
receipt		
ceiling		
received		

Watch out for exceptions:

neither   their   leisure   seize   neighbours   reign
weighing   eight

CHALLENGE TWELVE

SPELLING RULE NUMBER THIRTEEN

Zoggy says,

"BE AWARE OF WORDS WITH SILENT LETTERS."

Wrestle with my **kn**ees.

Wrestle with my **wr**ists.

LOOK OUT FOR THIS CHEEKY FELLOW: SILENT O

Read these words. Can you spell them?

c<u>o</u>untryside	d<u>o</u>uble	cautious	mysterious
fam<u>o</u>us	n<u>o</u>urish	precious	cousin
delicious	country	curious	victorious

you	route	youth	routine
tourist	troupe	coupon	tour
soup	group		

"Zoggy decides to run a cross country race."

Rule:

'ou' - 'o' is silent

'u' sounds like 'oo'

Time for a test.

READ	COPY	COVER & SPELL
knowledge		
wrong		
wrist		
climbed		
wreck		
wrap		
knife		
answer		
comb		
climb		
gnome		
knight		
gnaw		
knocked		
ghost		
crumb		
thumb		
knitting		
knew		
know		
numb		
lamb		

Remember silent letters.
Underline the silent letters in each word. Can you find the silent letter in these words? sign, hour, calm, column

CHALLENGE THIRTEEN

IS ZOGGY **ROUGH AND TOUGH** ENOUGH FOR THE BOXING RING?

"1, 2, 3, 4, 5, 6, 7, 8, 9, 10... punches."

He fought and he fought but he was brought down by his opponent.

Zoggy is thoughtful. There are few sporting opportunities on Planet Zen and he does not think he will ever become a famous, courageous and victorious sports-alien. In fact, he is terrible at sports but he is good at spelling!

"Are you rough and tough enough to learn words with OUGH and AUGH?"

ought	bought	brought	fought
thought	nought	tough	rough
enough	cough	trough	plough
bough	caught	taught	daughter
laugh	slaughter	thorough	thoroughly
dough	although		

Sort the words into two groups.

AU	OU
taught	ought

Time for a test.

READ	COPY	COVER & SPELL
mouthful		
delightful		
thoughtful		
beautiful		
useful		
fearful		
suitable		
peaceful		
honourable		
comfortable		
available		
marvellous		
enormous		
mischievous		
famous		
generous		
famous		
previous		
gracious		
industrious		
spacious		
suspicious		
furious		
victorious		

Remember: long words have one 'l' e.g. beautiful
Listen to the sounds and learn which words have 'ble', 'able', 'ous' and 'ious'.

CHALLENGE FOURTEEN

Zoggy attends a big sporting celebration and helps you learn some harder word patterns.

"THE OLYMPICS!"

Imag**ine** the surp**rise** on Zoggy's face when he **acq**uires a ticket to gain adm**ission** to a big sporting celebra**tion**!

He will be a spect**ator** at the opening performance.

Can you spell the underlined words?

Time for a test.

READ	COPY	COVER & SPELL
compare		
improve		
reverse		
imagine		
surprise		
exercise		
advertise		
disguise		
procession		
discussion		
separation		
exhibition		
celebration		
occupation		
preparation		
question		
acquire		
acquaintance		
earthquake		
acquaint		

What have we found out about Zoggy's character?

	YES	NO
Is he obstin<u>ate</u>?		
Is he a priv<u>ate</u> person?		
Does he like chocol<u>ate</u>?		
Can he play crick<u>et</u>?		
Does he chuck<u>le</u>?		
Does he gru<u>mble</u>?		
Does he trav<u>el</u> like an ang<u>el</u>?		
Is he speci<u>al</u>, comic<u>al</u>, practic<u>al</u>?		
Is he ma<u>gical</u>?		
Is he a creat<u>ure</u> that is full of advent<u>ure</u>?		
Does he cope with pres<u>sure</u>?		
Does he get into disc<u>ussions</u>?		

Look at the endings underlined. Can you spell these words?

WHAT IS AN ALIEN LIKE?

Is he <u>bright</u>?
Does he <u>fight</u>?

Is he <u>grotesque</u>?
Is he <u>unique</u>?

Does he read a <u>magazine</u>?
Jump on a <u>trampoline</u>?

Join a <u>league</u>?
Is he full of <u>intrigue</u>?

Does he ride an <u>elephant</u>?
Or swim with the <u>dolphins</u>?

Go to the <u>chemist</u>
For pills for his <u>stomach</u>?

Can he explain <u>ancient</u> myths?
Can he dive deep in the <u>ocean</u>

Does he have <u>special</u> powers?
Does he <u>swallow</u> down <u>warmed waffles</u>?

Does our world fill him with <u>amusement</u>?
Does it fill him with <u>astonishment</u>?

Does he like to <u>walk</u>?
Does he like to look at <u>wonderful scenery</u>?

Does he like <u>salt</u>
Or <u>biscuits</u> with <u>malt</u>?

Would he prefer to eat <u>fruit</u>
Or food that's good <u>value</u>?

Does he <u>listen</u> to music?
Does he know any <u>Martians</u>?

Is he <u>cautious</u>?
Is he <u>patient</u>?

"Look at the underlined words."

Time for a test.

READ	COPY	COVER & SPELL
assistance		
ignorance		
attendance		
performance		
entrance		
commence		
absence		
pretence		
audience		
obedience		
prophet		
cricket		
blanket		
bracelet		
obstinate		
private		
chocolate		
skeleton		
heaven		
reason		

CHALLENGE FIFTEEN

Zoggy's last challenge...

Zoggy says,

"LEARN HOMOPHONES"

Words that sound the same but have different spellings and meanings.

The girl read the red book.

Zoggy says,

"LEARN HOMONYMS"

Words with the same spelling, but different meanings.

The dog who had a loud bark, scratches the bark of the tree.

HEARD / HERD

Zoggy heard the cheers of the crowd. No, it was a herd of cows.

GROAN / GROWN

Zoggy groans because he is exhausted from running the race.

The plant had grown.

HIGHER / HIRE

Zoggy jumps higher.

He wants to hire an earth car.

KEY / QUAY

Zoggy opens his space ship door with a key.

He walks to look at the sailing boats in the quay.

MISSED / MIST

Zoggy missed the earth bus because he was lost in the mist.

BOY / BUOY

Zoggy makes friends with an earth boy.

A buoy marks where the boats can sail.

KNOWS / NOSE

Zoggy <u>knows</u> how to spell all words.

Earth people smell with their <u>noses</u>.

KNIGHT / NIGHT

Earth people sleep at <u>night</u>.

<u>Knights</u> wear armour and joust on horseback.

MALE / MAIL

The <u>male</u> horse is a stallion.

The postman delivers the <u>mail</u>.

PALE / PAIL

Zoggy goes <u>pale</u> when he sees a monster.

He puts a <u>pail</u> under the leaking roof.

LIGHTENING / LIGHTNING

There was a flash of <u>lightning</u>.

Auntie Joe is <u>lightening</u> her hair.

MARE / MAYOR

A female horse is a <u>mare</u>.

The mayor, wearing his gold chain, opened the fair.

PEAL / PEEL

Zoggy heard a <u>peal</u> of bells, while he <u>peeled</u> the vegetables.

ROME / ROAM

Zoggy <u>roamed</u> along the streets of the city of <u>Rome</u>.

SEEM / SEAM

The <u>seam</u> of Zoggy's space suit <u>seems</u> to have come unstitched. How annoying!

PEACE / PIECE

Zoggy eats a <u>piece</u> of pie, in the <u>peace</u> of his garden.

WONDER / WANDER

Zoggy <u>wonders</u> what to do next, as he <u>wanders</u> down the street.

BREAK / BRAKE

The car <u>brakes</u> sharply.

The earth boy <u>breaks</u> his arm.

PAUSE / PAWS

The earth cat <u>pauses</u> for a moment and then licks his <u>paws</u>.

STRAIGHT / STRAIT

The boat sails <u>straight</u> along the <u>strait</u>.

NEW / KNEW

Zoggy <u>knew</u> he would get on well with his <u>new</u> earth friends.

PRAISE / PRAYS

Zoggy <u>prays</u> that he will win the race.

Teacher <u>praises</u> Zoggy for his good work.

COURT / CAUGHT

Zoggy <u>caught</u> a cold on the tennis <u>court</u>.

CAUSE / COURSE

The <u>cause</u> of the accident was not clear.

Of <u>course</u>, you can come to tea on Sunday.

WHERE WERE WEAR

Where were you on Friday Zoggy?

What did you wear for the party?

THERE THEIR THEY'RE

They're playing with their i-pads over there.

QUITE QUIET

It is quite quiet at night on earth.

TO TOO TWO

I went to a party.
I ate too much.
I had two cupcakes.

HERE HEAR

You can hear a dog howl over here.

FAIR / FARE

It is not _fair_ if I have to pay a _fare_ on the bus.

NOW / KNOW

I am very glad that I _know_ that secret _now_.

SAIL / SALE

Sail a boat.

Go to a clothes _sale_.

CREW / CRUISE

Join the _crew_ of a ship.

Go on a _cruise_.

DESERT / DESSERT

I ate an ice cream _dessert_, in the sandy _desert_.

RIGHT / WRITE

Get your maths _right_ and then _write_ a story.

BY / BUY

Go _by_ car. _Buy_ a computer.

GREAT / GRATE

Be _great_.

Grate some cheese.

TEACH / LEARN

The teacher <u>teaches</u> and I <u>learn</u>.

TALE / TAIL

A cat licks his <u>tail</u>.

Read a scary <u>tale</u>.

FATHER / FARTHER

An earth child calls his father Dad.

I will drive farther along the road.

STATIONARY / STATIONERY

Write a letter using my <u>stationery</u>.

In the traffic, all the cars are <u>stationary</u>.

SITE / SIGHT

Go to the building <u>site</u>.

Get my <u>sight</u> tested.

Try these:

1. Zoggy stayed in because of the .... (weather/whether).

2. He .... (rung/wrung) out his wet clothes.

3. He was bored and uttered a low .... (groan/grown).

4. There was thunder and .... (lightening/lightning) in the skies.

5. Does it .... (affect/effect) him?

6. He wants to live in .... (peace/piece) and he can't .... (wait/weight) for tomorrow.

Zoggy records some of his observations so he can report back to Planet Zen...

1. Humans have blood in their .... (veins/vains).

2. They eat .... (serial/cereal) for breakfast; it smells .... (fowl/foul) to Zoggy.

3. Birds called owls .... (pray/prey) on mice.

4. Some human houses have .... (cellars/sellers).

5. Rose plants in their gardens have a lovely .... (sent/scent).

6. The queen is the most important person and she sits on a .... (throne/thrown).

7. To ride a horse you hold the .... (reigns/reins).

8. Ancient people have ceremonies, which are called ancient .... (writes/rights/rites).

9. When earthlings go on holiday, they sometimes take a .... (crews/cruise).

10. Humans use a needle to .... (sew/sow) their clothes and cotton on .... (reels/reals).

Zoggy says,

Time for a test.

READ	COPY	COVER & SPELL
knowledge		
realistic		
grumble		
special		
amongst		
creature		
common		
slippery		
aware		
purpose		
anchor		
floated		
retreated		
flickering		
spreading		
flight		
supernatural		
steady		
charging		

Time for a test.

READ	COPY	COVER & SPELL
technique		
designed		
exterior		
journey		
materials		
freeze		
practise		
opposite		
mention		
banging		
centre		

Revision

1. Add five more words that end in 'y'.

	ADD 'ER'	ADD 'EST'
FRIENDLY	friendlier	friendliest
LOVELY	lovelier	loveliest

2. Magic 'e' makes the 'a' sound long. Double the consonant and add 'er' to make a sound short.

| fat | fate | | fat | fatter |
| mat | mate | **but** | mat | matter |

3. In words that end in 'er', the consonant is doubled. Can you think of five more words?

| ham | hammer | fat | fatter |

4. Read these words aloud. What do you notice?

| holy | holly | pupil | puppet |

5. Look at these:

wide	wider	widest
safe	safer	safest
thin	thinner	thinnest

6. Complete the following chart and add more words.

	ING	ED	ER
stop	stopping	stopped	stopper
wish	....	....	....
bake	baking	baked	baker
run	....	....	....
lock	locking	locked	locker

7. English words do not end in 'i' - 'macaroni' is an Italian word. Find some more examples.

8. Find some more examples. Add 'ly' and 'ily'.

LY	ILY
suddenly	happily
....	....
....	....

9. Find some more examples.

Y	IES	IED
cry	cries	cried
fry	fries	fried
....	....	....

10. Find five words for each sound.

TCH	DGE	IE	EI
ditch	edge	field	reign
		relief	neighbour
		thief	their

11. Sort the following words into five groups.

badge   sketch   ginger   sponge   circle
bandage   evidence   clutch   centre   circumference
giant   orange   generous   cygnet   gypsy
gentle   entrance   appearance   fudge   butcher
luggage   passage

TCH	DGE	GE,GI,GY	NGE	CE,CI,CY

12. What do you see?

lick   licking   like   liking

Underline the long vowel sounds in the following words.

able   trifle   stable

Underline short vowel sounds in the following words.

raffle   little   principle   struggle   puddle
incredible   susceptible inconceivable incredible

Add more words with short vowel sounds.

terrible   impossible   invisible   ....

Add more words with long vowel sounds.

stable   enable   ....

13. Underline silent letters in the following words.

    castle   wrestle   knowledge
    comb   whistle   wriggling

14. Find five more words ending in 'ness'.

    darkness   loneliness   ....

15. How many syllables are in the following words?

    umbrella =   establishment =

16. Find five more words with 'ough' and five with 'aught'.

    ought   bought   bough   ....
    daughter   haughty   ....

17. Find five words for the sounds 'au' and 'aw'.

    audition   awesome   ....

18. Find five words for the sounds 'ui' and 'ue'.

    fruit   juice   nuisance   blue   TRUE

19. Find more examples of words that add 'able'

    comfortable   ....

    believe ⟶ believable   (exceptions - noticeable and courageous)

20. Look for silent 'o' as 'ous'

    gorgeous   victorious   behaviour   honour   ....

21. Find five more words with the following prefixes:

RE	remain	refreshment	....
PRE	prevention	....	....
BE	before	become	....
IN	inedible	....	....
DE	descendent	....	....

22. Underline the silent letters in the following words (for example, the Greek 'ph' that sounds like 'f' and the 'ch' that sounds like 'ck').

crumble   gnash   wrong   gnome   deception

hymn   dumb   school   dolphin   chemist

elephant   nephew   Christmas

23. Find more words with the following suffixes and endings

MENT	astonishment	entertainment	....	....
LE	staple	....	....	....
EL	angel	....	....	....
IVE	expensive	....	....	....
GHT	lightning	fighting	....	....
TION	explanation	information	participation	inspiration
URE	capture	manufacture	adventure	furniture

24. What happens to these words when you add endings like 'sion'?

divide   division   miserable   miserably

explode   explosion   persuade   persuasion

succeed   succession   impress   impression

25. Find more words ending with sound 'ion'

    attention   *invention*   *inspection*

    education   *consideration*   *conversation*

26. Find more words with 'u' as in:

    tissue   *student*   *music*   *university*   ....

27. Find more words with the following sounds:

WA	want	waffle	warrior
QUA	quarantine	....	....

28. Read and find some more examples:

    'our' sounds like 'or' in pour/four   *'ou' sounds like 'oo' in soup/four*

    ough' sounds like 'off' in trough, 'uff' as in enough 'ow' as in plough, 'oh' as in although and 'ou' as in thoroughly   *'ci' and 'ti' as in special, influential, patient and precision*

    'wo' as in wonderful person

29. Find some more words for 'or', 'ar' and 'er'

OR	solicitor	author	....
AR	cellar	burglar	....
ER	divider	rider	....

30. Find some more words with a hard 'ch' sound.

    chemist   *anchor*   ....

Find some more words with a soft 'ch' sound like 'sh'

parachute ....

31. Find some more words with a short 'ive'

expensive *pensive* ....

Find some more words with a long 'ive'

survive *arrive* ....

32. Find some more words with the sound 'que'

unique *picturesque* ....

33. Drop e...

visible *visibility* *preferable* *preferably*

....

34. Find more words with the sound 'ent'

parliament *obedient* *government* *convenient* ....

35. 'or', 'ar', 'er'?

profess............ *schol*............ *lawy*............

36.

excel *excellent* ....

37. 'ible' or 'able'

irresist............ *poss*............

Get an adult to check your answers or look in a dictionary.

FINAL TESTS

READ	COPY	COVER & SPELL
lightning		
raining		
coastal		
height		
weight		
unnerve		
gorge		
physical		
psychology		
debt		
subtle		
photograph		
yacht		
humorous		
accommodate		
mischievous		
privilege		
disastrous		
marvellous		

FINAL TEST

READ	COPY	COVER & SPELL
gnome		
ghostly		
phantom		
knight		
enemies		
receipt		
persuasive		
aisle		
thistle		
suspense		
believe		
concert		
perceive		
weird		
principle		
protein		
miscellaneous		
separate		
accommodate		
pronunciation		

READ	COVER & SPELL	READ	COVER & SPELL
moon		morning	
cool		report	
roomy		before	
seemed		visitor	
greenery		solicitor	
cookery		grasshopper	
booked		baker	
looked		letter	
weeks		butter	
feeding		pepper	
turning		amuse	
curled		refuse	
disturb		computer	
Thursday		stripes	
furnish		excuse	
skirt		value	
thirty		refrain	
dirty		drain	
thirsty		exclaim	
whirling		Spain	
carpet		upstairs	
party		Sunday	
hardly		holiday	
depart		crayon	
market			

READ	COVER & SPELL
family	
yellow	
yesterday	
pyramid	
system	
reply	
deny	
python	
multiply	
qualify	
glowing	
throwing	
snow ball	
crow	
flown	
groan	
roast	
toast	
soap	
boat	
please	
reason	
breathe	
leave	
beneath	
appear	
near	

READ	COVER & SPELL
instead	
dreadful	
weather	
feather	
spread	
healthy	
paw	
awful	
draw	
straw	
trawler	
automatic	
haunted	
laundry	
audience	
Autumn	
August	
creepy crawly	
brown	
clown	
flower	
power	
towel	
shout	
trousers	
count	
cloud	

READ	COVER & SPELL
woodlouse	
newspaper	
blew	
sewing	
grew	
few	
true	
tissue	
value	

TIME FOR A TEST

haunted	shouted	treading	audience
mountain	awaiting	laundry	borrow
crawl	corner	elbow	awkward
explore	because	awful	together
consider	caught	flour	reading
perform	coward	autumn	encounter
August	windows	automobile	cloudy
noisy			

Remember: use **phonic sounds** to sound out words.

ch, sh, th , wh, oo, ee, 'e', or, ar, er, ur, ir, oa, ai, ay, oi, oy, y (like e or i), ou, ow, au, aw, ce, age, ue, ew

Zoggy's Spelling Lists

AR		EL		AL	
probable	miserable	novel	marvel	special	national
terrible	freckle	camel	shovel	magical	arrival
cuddle	crackle	label	quarrel	medical	hospital
tickle	middle	parcel	channel	comical	
buckle	incredible	panel	tunnel	practical	
possible	bundle	cancel	squirrel	musical	
simple	grumble	angel	quarrel	physical	
chuckle	gentle	travel		fanatical	
bottle	knuckle	model		punctual	

URE		ION		S ION	
lure	figure	station	explanation	cushion	tension
mixture	pressure	decoration	collection	passion	
picture	furniture	population	protection	Russian	
nature	adventure	education	attraction	suspension	
failure	injure	consideration	preparation	procession	
capture	manure	conversation	inspection	discussion	
puncture		association	mention	compassion	
creature		prescription	examination	admission	
texture		information	ventilation	percussion	
rupture		sensation	exhibition	permission	
future		administration	congregation	pension	

FUL		IBLE		ABLE	
beautiful	delightful	responsible	impossible	available	miserable
delightful	mouthful	edible	invisible	peaceable	comfortable
thoughtful	hateful	sensible		honourable	

OUS		IOUS		AGE	
famous	mischievous	spacious	precious	discourage	average
generous		industrious	suspicious	advantage	manage
delicious		furious		carriage	

Complete:

burgl...   *popular*   *caretaker*   *disaster*   *caland...*

similar   *radiat...*   *interi...*   *author*   *rememb...*

lawyer   *passing*   *conqueror*   *governor*

ENCE	ANCE	ILL
obedience absence audience	assistance performance ignorance	ill illegal illustration illuminate illegible

WA	SHORT Y	LONG Y
water waddle warrant warrior wander	typical hymn	hygiene hyacinth hydrate hyphen type tyrant

QUE	PH	OU	
plague fatigue league catalogue monologue	elephant physical psychiatrist photograph	rough tough enough cough thought	thorough youth round troupe group

EI	AU		OU	
height freight eighty weight	caught haughty daughter slaughter	draught	young noun cousin southern	trouble country fountain thousand

SC		QU	SILENT SOUNDS	
ascend scientist descend scissors scent	sceptre scientist science scenery	quay queue quarrel qualification question	knuckle stomach tongue design solemn wrestle	knowledge exhibition salmon psalm autumn

squawk awkward trawler lawyer crawly	lorries monkeys jockeys hobbies donkeys	receipt impossible leisure explosion neighbour dismissal assistance

autumn tarpaulin audience saucer haunted	hoped hopped scrapped scraped whining winning	surprise exercise advertise concise precise

maintain appreciate complain tomorrow exclaiming shelter portrait payment essay	clap plan clapping planning slip slipping	improve imagine improving imagining arrange arranging

GHT	QUE	INE
light bright fight — Would he get into a fight?	cheque antique picturesque — Is he unique? grotesque	magazine trampoline Aunt Pauline — Can he jump high on a trampoline? tangerine margarine

GUE	PH	HARD CH
catalogue league intrigue — Join a basketball league? dialogue	phrase Uncle Philip pharmacy telephone photography Sophie pheasant phantom elephant dolphin	stomach Nicholas character chorus school chemist echo Christmas

WA	S', 'C' CAN SOUND LIKE:	
want watching wanting warrior what warning waffle swarm swallow reward waddle backwards warrant	sugar ocean sure ancient insure precious insurance delicious pressure special	Remember: sometimes English words are difficult. Some words have tricky endings 'ght' e.g. light. 'ine' can sound like 'een' e.g. machine

MENT		QUA		AL	
astonishment	amendment	quarter	quickly	walk	fault
entertainment	agreement	quarantine	quietly	stalk	salt
employment	argument	quarrel	squashed	chalk	bald
arrangement	punishment	squabble	quadruple	small	malt
amusement		squadron	qualify	wall	
improvement		quarry	question	halt	

SE		WOR		UIT	
ascend	scenery	worship	worm	biscuit	bruise
descend		worthless	wonderful	fruit	
science		worst		recruit	
scientist		world		cruise	
scissors		working		nuisance	
sceptre		workman		suiit	

UE		SILENT ST			
blue	value	bustle	bomb	cautious	
rescue	student	whistle	comb	patient	
true	music	castle	thumb	initial	
statue	tube	listen		essential	
tissue	university			martian	

www.ingramcontent.com/pod-product-compliance
Lightning Source LLC
Chambersburg PA
CBHW050715090526
44587CB00019B/3382